REPORT

FROM THE

DEPARTMENT OF STATE

IN RELATION TO THE

CONDITION OF THE COMMERCIAL RELATIONS

BETWEEN THE

UNITED STATES AND THE SPANISH-AMERICAN STATES.

TRANSMITTED TO THE SENATE IN OBEDIENCE TO A RESOLUTION.

WASHINGTON.
GOVERNMENT PRINTING OFFICE.
1870.

REPORT

FROM THE

DEPARTMENT OF STATE

IN RELATION TO THE

CONDITION OF THE COMMERCIAL RELATIONS

BETWEEN THE

UNITED STATES AND THE SPANISH-AMERICAN STATES.

TRANSMITTED TO THE SENATE IN OBEDIENCE TO A RESOLUTION.

WASHINGTON.
GOVERNMENT PRINTING OFFICE.
1870.

CORRESPONDENCE.

DEPARTMENT OF STATE,
Washington, July 14, 1870.

The Secretary of State, to whom was referred the resolution of the Senate requesting the President "to institute an inquiry, by such means as in his judgment shall be deemed proper, into the present condition of the commercial relations between the United States and the Spanish-American states on this continent, and between those countries and other nations, and to communicate to the Senate full and complete statements regarding the same, together with such recommendations as he may think necessary to promote the development and increase of our commerce with those regions, and to secure to the United States that proportionate share of the trade of this continent to which their close relations of geographical contiguity and political friendship with all the states of America justly entitle them," has the honor to report:

The resolution justly regards the commercial and the political relations of the United States with the American states of Spanish origin. as necessarily dependent upon each other. If the commerce of those countries has been diverted from its natural connection with the United States, the fact may probably be partly traced to political causes, which have been swept away by the great civil convulsion in this country.

For the just comprehension of the position of this government in the American political system, and for the causes which have failed to give it hitherto the influence to which it is properly entitled, by reason of its democratic system, and of the moderation and sense of justice which have distinguished its foreign policy through successive administrations from the birth of the nation until now, it is necessary to make a brief notice of such measures as affect our present relations to the other parts of this continent.

The United States were the first of the European colonies in America to arrive at maturity as a people, and assume the position of an independent republic. Since then important changes have taken place in various nations and in every part of the world. Our own growth in power has been not the least remarkable of all the great events of modern history.

When, at the conclusion of the revolutionary war, having conquered by arms our right to exist as a sovereign state, that right was at length recognized by treaties, we occupied only a narrow belt of land along the Atlantic coast, hemmed in at the north, the west, and the south by the possessions of European governments, or by uncultivated wastes beyond the Alleghanies, inhabited only by the aborigines. But, in the very infancy of the United States, far-sighted statesmen saw and predicted that, weak in population and apparently restricted in available territory as the new republic then was, it had within it the germs of colossal grandeur, and would, at no remote day, occupy the continent of America with its institutions, its authority, and its peaceful influence.

That expectation has been thus far signally verified. The United States entered at once into the occupation of their rightful possessions westward to the banks of the Mississippi. Next, by the spontaneous proffer of France, they acquired Louisiana and its territorial extension, or right of extension, north to the line of the treaty demarcation between France and Great Britain, and west to the Pacific Ocean. Next, by amicable arrangement with Spain, they acquired the Floridas, and complete southern maritime frontiers upon the Gulf of Mexico. Then came the union with the independent State of Texas, followed by the acquisitions of California and New Mexico, and then of Arizona. Finally, Russia has ceded to us Alaska, and the continent of North America has become independent of Europe, except so much of it as continues to maintain political relations with Great Britain.

Meanwhile, partly by natural increase, and partly by voluntary immigration from Europe, our population has risen from three millions to nearly forty millions; the number of States and Territories united under the Constitution has been augmented from thirteen to forty-seven; the development of internal wealth and power has kept pace with political expansion; we have occupied in part and peopled the vast interior of the continent; we have bound the Pacific to the Atlantic by a chain of intervening States and organized Territories; we have delivered the republic from the anomaly and the ignominy of domestic servitude; we have constitutionally fixed the equality of all races and of all men before the law; and we have established, at the cost of a great civil war—a cost, however, not beyond the value of such a result—the indissoluble national unity of the United States.

In all these marked stages of national progress, from the Declaration of Independence to the recent amendments of the Constitution, it is impossible not to perceive a providential series and succession of events, intimately attached, one to the other, and possessed of definite character as a whole, whatever incidental departures from such uniformity may have marked or seemed to mark our foreign policy under the influence of temporary causes, or of the conflicting opinions of statesmen.

In the time of Washington, of the first Adams, of Jefferson, and of Madison, the condition of Europe, engaged in the gigantic wars of the French revolution and of the empire, produced its series of public questions, and gave tone and color to our foreign policy. In the time of Monroe, of the second Adams, and of Jackson, and subsequently thereto, the independence of the Spanish and Portuguese colonies of America produced its series of questions and its apparent modification of our public policy. Domestic questions of territorial organization, of social emancipation, and of national unity have also largely occupied the minds and the attention of the later administrations.

The treaties of alliance and guarantee with France which contributed so much to our independence, were one source of solicitude to the early administrations, which were endeavoring to protect our commerce from the depredations and wrongs to which the maritime policy of England and the reaction of that policy on France subjected it. For twenty years we struggled in vain to accomplish this, and at last drifted into war.

The avoidance of entangling alliances, the characteristic feature of the foreign policy of Washington, sprang from this condition of things. But the entangling alliances which then existed were engagements made with France as a part of the general contract under which aid was furnished to us for the achievement of our independence. France was willing to waive the letter of the obligation as to her West India possessions, but demanded, in its stead, privileges in our ports which the administration was unwilling to concede. To make its refusal acceptable to a public which sympathized with France, the cabinet of General Washington exaggerated the principle into a theory tending to national isolation.

The public measures designed to maintain unimpaired the domestic sovereignty and the international neutrality of the United States were independent of this policy, though apparently incidental to it. The municipal laws enacted by Congress then and since have been but declarations of the law of nations. They are essential to the preservation of our national dignity and honor; they have for their object to repress and punish all enterprises of private war, one of the last relics of mediæval barbarism; and they have descended to us from the fathers of the republic, supported and enforced by every succeeding President of the United States.

The foreign policy of these early days was not a narrow one. During this period we secured the evacuation by Great Britain of the country wrongfully occupied by her on the lakes; we acquired Louisiana; we measured forces on the sea with France, and on the land and sea with England; we set the example of resisting and chastising the piracies of the Barbary States; we initiated in negotiations with Prussia the long line of treaties for the liberalization of war and the promotion of international intercourse; and we steadily demanded, and at length obtained, indemnification from various governments for the losses we had suffered by foreign spoliations in the wars of Europe.

To this point in our foreign policy we had arrived when the revolutionary movements in Spanish and Portuguese America compelled a modification of our relations with Europe, in consequence of the rise of new and independent states in America.

The revolution which commenced in 1810, and extended through all the Spanish American continental colonies, after vain efforts of repression on the part of Spain, protracted through twenty years, terminated in the establishment of the independent states of Mexico, Guatemala, San Salvador, Honduras, Nicaragua, Costa Rica, Venezuela, Colombia, Ecuador, Peru, Chili, Bolivia, the Argentine Republic, Uruguay, and Paraguay, to which the empire of Brazil came in time to be added. These events necessarily enlarged the sphere of action of the United States, and essentially modified our relations with Europe, and our attitude to the rest of this continent.

The new states were, like ourselves, revolted colonies. They continued the precedent we had set, of separating from Europe. Their assumption of independence was stimulated by our example. They professedly imitated us, and copied our national Constitution, sometimes even to their inconvenience.

The Spanish-American colonies had not the same preparation for independence that we had. Each of the British colonies possessed complete local autonomy. Its formal transition from dependence to independence consisted chiefly in expelling the British governor of the colony, and electing a governor of the State, from which to the organized Union was but a step. All these conditions of success were wanting in Spanish America, and hence many of the difficulties in their career as independent states; and, further, while the revolution in British America was the exclusive result of the march of opinion in the British colonies, the simultaneous action of the separate Spanish colonies, though showing a desire for independence, was principally produced by the accident of the invasion of Spain by France.

The formation of these new sovereignties in America was important to us, not only because of the cessation of colonial monopolies to that extent, but because of the geographical relations to us, held by so many new nations, all, like ourselves, created from European stock, and interested in excluding European politics, dynastic questions, and balances of power from further influence in the New World.

Thus the United States were forced into new lines of action, which, though apparently in some respects conflicting, were really in harmony with the line marked out by Washington. The avoidance of entangling political alliances, and the maintenance of our own independent neutrality became doubly important from the fact that they became applicable to the new republics as well as to the mother country. The duty of non-interference had been admitted by every President. The question came up in the time of the first Adams, on the occasion of the enlistment projects of Miranda. It appeared again under Jefferson (anterior to the revolt of the Spanish colonies) in the schemes of Aaron Burr. It was an ever present question in the administrations of Madison, Monroe, and the younger Adams, in reference to the questions of foreign enlistment or equipment in the United States, and when these new republics entered the family of nations, many of them very feeble, and all too much subect to internal revolution and civil war, a strict adherence to our previous policy and a strict enforcement of our laws became essential to the preservation of friendly relations with them; for, since that time, it has been one of the principal cares of those intrusted with the administration of the government, to prevent piratical expeditions against these sister republics from leaving our ports. And thus the changed condition of the New World made no change in the traditional and peaceful policy of the United States in this respect.

In one respect, however, the advent of these new states in America did compel an apparent change of foreign policy on our part. It devolved upon us the determination of the great international question, at what time, and under what circumstances, to recognize a new power as entitled to a place among the family of nations. There was but little of precedent to guide us, except our own case. Something, indeed, could be inferred from the historical origin of the Netherlands and Switzerland. But our own case, carefully and conscientiously considered, was sufficient to guide us to right conclusions. We maintained our position of international friendship and of treaty obligations toward Spain, but we did not consider that we were bound to wait for its recognition of the new republics before admitting them into treaty relations with us as sovereign States. We held that it was for us to judge whether or not they had attained to the condition of actual independence, and the consequent right of recognition by us. We considered this question of fact deliberately and coolly. We sent commissioners to Spanish America to ascertain and report for our information concerning their actual circumstances, and in the fullness of time we acknowledged their independence; we exchanged diplomatic ministers, and made treaties of amity with them, the earliest of which, negotiated by Mr. John Quincy Adams, served as the model for the subsequent treaties with the Spanish-American republics. We also, simultaneously therewith, exerted our good offices with Spain, to induce her to submit to the inevitable result, and herself to accept and acknowledge the independence of her late colonies. We endeavored to induce Russia to join us in these representations. In all this our action was positive, in the direction of promoting the complete political separation of America from Europe.

A vast field was thus opened to the statesmen of the United States for the peaceful introduction, the spread, and the permanent establishment of the American ideas of republican government, of modification of the laws of war, of liberalization of commerce, of religious freedom and toleration, and of the emancipation of the New World from the dynastic and balance of power controversies of Europe.

Mr. John Quincy Adams, beyond any other statesman of the time in this country, had the knowledge and experience, both European and American, the comprehension of thought and purpose, and the moral convictions which peculiarly fitted him to introduce our country into this new field, and to lay the foundation of an American policy. The declaration known as the Monroe doctrine, and the objects and purposes of the congress of Panama, both supposed to have been largely inspired by Mr. Adams, have influenced public events from that day to this, as a principle of government for this continent and its adjacent islands.

It was at the period of the congress of Aix-la-Chapelle and of Laybach, when the "holy alliance" was combined to arrest all political changes in Europe in the sense of liberty, when they were intervening in Southern Europe for the re-establishment of absolutism, and when they were meditating interference to check the progress of free government in America, that Mr. Monroe, in his annual message of December, 1823, declared that the United States would consider any attempt to extend the European system to any portion of this hemisphere as dangerous to our peace and safety. "With the existing colonies or dependencies of any European power," he said, "we have not interfered and shall not interfere. But with the governments who have declared their independence, and maintained it, and whose independence we have on great consideration and on just principles acknowledged, we could not view any interposition for the purpose of oppressing them, or controlling, in any other manner, their destiny, by any European power, in any other light than as the manifestation of an unfriendly feeling towards the United States."

This declaration resolved the solution of the immediate question of the independence of the Spanish American colonies, and is supposed to have exercised some influence upon the course of the British cabinet in regard to the absolutist schemes in Europe as well as in America.

It has also exercised a permanent influence on this continent. It was at once invoked in consequence of the supposed peril of Cuba on the side of Europe; it was applied to a similar danger threatening Yucatan; it was embodied in the treaty of the United States and Great Britain as to Central America; it produced the successful opposition of the United States to the attempt of Great Britain to exercise dominion in Nicaragua under the cover of the Mosquito Indians; and it operated in like manner to prevent the establishment of a European dynasty in Mexico.

The United States stand solemnly committed by repeated declarations and repeated acts to this doctrine, and its application to the affairs of this continent. In his message to the two Houses of Congress at the commencement of the present session, the President, following the teachings of all our history, said that the existing "dependencies are no longer regarded as subject to transfer from one European power to another. When the present relation of colonies ceases, they are to become independent powers, exercising the right of choice and of self-control in the determination of their future condition and relations with other powers."

This policy is not a policy of aggression; but it opposes the creation of European dominion on American soil, or its transfer to other European powers, and it looks hopefully to the time when, by the voluntary departure of European governments from this continent and the adjacent islands, America shall be wholly American.

It does not contemplate forcible intervention in any legitimate contest; but it protests against permitting such a contest to result in the increase of European power or influence; and it ever impels this government, as in the late contest between the South American republics and Spain, to interpose its good offices to secure an honorable peace.

The congress of Panama was planned by Bolivar to secure the union of Spanish America against Spain. It had originally military as well as political purposes. In the military objects the United States could take no part; and indeed the necessity for such objects ceased when the full effects of Mr. Monroe's declarations were felt. But the pacific objects of the Congress, the establishment of close and cordial relations of amity, the creation of commercial intercourse, of interchange of political thought, and of habits of good understanding between the new republics and the United States and their respective citizens, might perhaps have been attained, had the administration of that day received the united support of the country. Unhappily they were lost; the new states were removed from the sympathetic and protecting influence of our example, and their commerce, which we might then have secured, passed into other hands, unfriendly to the United States.

In looking back upon the Panama congress from this length of time, it is easy to understand why the earnest and patriotic men who endeavored to crystallize an American system for this continent failed.

Mr. Clay and Mr. Adams were far-sighted statesmen, but unfortunately they struck against the rock of African slavery. One of the questions proposed for discussion in the conference was "The consideration of the means to be adopted for the entire abolition of the African slave trade," to which proposition the committee of the United States Senate of that day replied, "The United States have not certainly the right, and ought never to feel the inclination, to dictate to others who may differ with them upon this subject, nor do the committee see the expediency of insulting other states with whom we are maintaining relations of perfect amity, by ascending the moral chair, and proclaiming from thence mere abstract principles, of the rectitude of which each nation enjoys the perfect right of deciding for itself." The same committee also alluded to the possibility that the condition of the islands of Cuba and Porto Rico, still the possessions of Spain, and still slaveholding, might be made the subject of discussion and of contemplated action by the Panama congress. "If ever the United States [they said] permit themselves to be associated with these nations in any general congress assembled for the discussion of common plans in any way affecting European interests, they will, by such act, not only deprive themselves of the ability they now possess of rendering useful assistance to the other American states, but also produce other effects prejudicial to their own interests."

Thus the necessity at that day of preserving the great interest of the southern States in African slavery, and of preventing a change in the character of labor in the islands of Cuba and Porto Rico, lost to the United States the opportunity of giving a permanent direction to the political and commercial connections ofthe newly enfranchised Spanish-American states, and their trade passed into hands unfriendly to the United States, and has remained there ever since.

Events, subsequent to that date, have tended to place us in a position to retrieve our mistakes; among which events may be particularly named the suppression of the rebellion, the manifestation of our undeveloped and unexpected military power, the retirement of the French from Mexico, and the abolition of slavery in the United States.

There is good reason to believe that the latter fact has had an important influence in our favor in Spanish America. It has caused us to be regarded there with more sympathetic as well as more respectful consideration. It has relieved those republics from the fear of fillibusterism which had been formerly incited against Central America and Mexico in the interest of slave extension; and it has produced an impression of the stability of our institutions and of our public strength sufficient to dissipate the fears of our friends or the hopes of those who wish us ill.

Thus there exists in the Spanish-American republics confidence toward the United States. On our side they find a feeling of cordial amity and friendship, and a desire to cultivate and develop our common interests on this continent. With some of these states our relations are more intimate than with others, either by reason of closer similarity of constitutional forms, of greater commercial intercourse, of proximity in fact, or of the construction or contemplated construction of lines of transit for our trade and commerce between the Atlantic and the Pacific. With several of them we have peculiar treaty relations. The treaty of 1846 between the United States and New Grenada contains stipulations of guaranty for the neutrality of that part of the Isthmus within the present territory of Colombia, and for the protection of the rights of sovereignty and property therein belonging to Colombia. Similar stipulations appear in the treaty of 1867 with Nicaragua, and of July, 1864, with Honduras. Those treaties (like the treaty of alliance made with France in 1778 by Dr. Franklin, Silas Deane, and Arthur Lee) constitute *pro tanto* a true protective alliance between the United States and each of those republics. Provisions of like effect appear in the treaty of April 19, 1850, between Great Britain and the United States.

Brazil, with her imperial semblance and constitutional reality, has always held relations of amity with us, which have been fortified by the opening of her great rivers to commerce. It needs only that, in emulation of Russia and the United States, she should emancipate her slaves, to place her in more complete sympathy with the rest of America.

It will not be presumptuous after the foregoing sketch to say, with entire consideration for the sovereignty and national pride of the Spanish American republics, that the United States, by the priority of their independence, by the stability of their institutions, by the regard of their people for the forms of law, by their resources as a government, by their naval power, by their commercial enterprise, by the attractions which they offer to European immigration, by the prodigious internal development of their resources and wealth, and by the intellectual life of their population, occupy of necessity a prominent position on this continent which they neither can nor should abdicate, which entitles them to a leading voice, and which imposes upon them duties of right and of honor regarding American questions, whether those questions affect emancipated colonies, or colonies still subject to European dominion.

The public questions which existed as to all European colonies, prior to and during the revolutions in the continental colonies of Spain and Portugal, still exist with reference to the European colonies which remain; and they now return upon us in full force, as we watch events in Cuba and Porto Rico.

Whatever may be the result of the pending contest in Cuba, it appears to be the belief of some of the leading statesmen of Spain, that the relations which now exist between the island and the mother country cannot be long continued. It is understood that the resources for carrying on the struggle have been supplied mainly from Cuba, by the aid of that portion of the population which does not desire to see its political destinies intrusted to the persons who direct the movements of the insurgents; but it does not follow that its political relations with Spain are to remain unchanged, or that even the party which is now dominant in the island will wish to forever continue colonists.

These facts give reason to think that, when the contest shall close, Cuba, with her resources strained, but unexhausted, (whatever may be her political relations,) will resume and continue her old commercial relations with the United States; and it is not impossible that at some day not far distant, when measured by the course of history, she will be called upon to elect her position in the family of nations.

Although the resolution of the Senate does not in terms apply to the Islands of the Antilles, it is impossible to answer it without speaking of them. They outlie the southern coast of the United States and guard the approaches to the ports of Mexico, Venezuela, and the Isthmus, by which we reach from the east the western coasts of Mexico and of the Spanish states. The people of the Spanish islands speak the language and share the traditions, customs, ideas, and religion of the Spanish American states of the continent, and will probably, like them, become, at some time, independent of the mother country. It would, therefore, be unwise, while shaping a commercial policy for the continent, to disregard the islands which lie so much nearer to our seaports.

With the Spanish islands of Cuba and Porto Rico we maintain, in spite of their adverse legislation, a large commerce by reason of our necessities and of their proximity. In the year ending June 30, 1869, we imported from them merchandise valued at $65,609,274. During the same time we sent them goods to the value only of $15,313,919.

The prohibitory duties forced upon them by the policy of Spain shut out much that we might supply. Their tropical productions, for instance, are too valuable to allow their lands to be given up to the growth of bread-stuffs; yet, instead of taking these articles from the superabundant fields of their nearest neighbors, they are forced to go to the distant plains of Spain. It will be for the interest of the United States to shape its general policy so that this relation of imports and exports shall be altered in Cuba when peace is restored and its political condition is satisfactorily established.

With none of the other Spanish American states in North and South America are our commercial relations what they should be. Our total imports in the year ending June 30, 1869, from these countries were less than $25,000,000, (or not one-half the amount from Cuba alone,) and our exports for the same time to them were only $17,850,313; and yet these countries have an aggregate population nearly or quite as great as that of the United States; they have republican forms of government, and they profess to be, and probably really are, in political sympathy with us.

This department is not able to give with entire accuracy the imports and exports of Great Britain with the same countries during the corresponding period. It is believed, however, the following figures will be found to be not far from correct:

Imports to Great Britain, $42,820,942; Exports from Great Britain, $40,682,102.

It thus appears that notwithstanding the greater distance which the commerce has to travel in coming to and from Great Britain, notwithstanding the political sympathy which ought naturally to exist between republics, notwithstanding the American idea which has been so prominently and so constantly put forward by the government of the United States, notwithstanding the acknowledged skill of American manufactures, notwithstanding the ready markets which the great cities of the United States afford for the consumption of tropical productions, the inhabitants of the Spanish-American continent consume of the products of Great Britain more than twice the quantity they take of the products of the United States, and that they sell to us only three-fifths of the amount they sell to Great Britain.

The Secretary of State appends to this report the tables on which these statements are founded. That their commerce with the United States is not large, may be partially explained by the fact that these states have been subject to many successive revolutions since the failure of the congress of Panama. These revolutions not only exhaust their resources and burden them with debt, but they check emigration, prevent the flow of foreign capital into the country, and stop the enterprise which needs a stable government for its development.

These suggestions are, however, applicable to the British commerce as well as to our own, and they do not explain why we, with the natural advantages in our favor, fall so far behind. The Isthmus of Panama is the common point where the commerce of the western coasts of Mexico and South America meets. When it arrives there, why should it seek Liverpool and London rather than New York?

The political causes which have operated to divert this commerce from us the Secretary of State has endeavored to explain. A favorable time has now come for removing them—for laying the foundation of an American policy which shall bind in closer union the American republics. Let them understand that the United States do not covet their territories; that our only desire is to see them peaceful, with free and stable governments, increasing in wealth and population, and developing in the lines in which their own traditions, customs, habits, laws, and modes of thought will naturally take them. Let them feel that, as in 1826, so now, this government is ready to aid them to the full extent of its constitutional power in any steps which they may take for their better protection against anarchy. Let them be convinced that the United States is prepared, in good faith and without ulterior purposes, to join them in the development of a peaceful American commercial policy, that may in time include this continent and the West Indian Islands. Let this be comprehended, and there will be no political reason why we may not "secure to the United States that proportionate share of the trade of this continent to which their close relations of geographical contiguity and political friendship with all the States of America justly entitle them."

It may not be enough to remove the political obstacles only. The financial policy which the war made necessary may have operated injuriously upon our commerce with these states. The resolution of the Senate calls, on these points, for detailed information which is not within the control of the Secretary of State, and for recommendations for the future which he is not prepared to give without that information. To fully answer the Senate's call, it would probably be necessary to employ some competent agent, familiar with the Spanish American states, to collate and arrange the information asked for; for this there is no appropriation by Congress.

Respectfully submitted.

HAMILTON FISH.

Commerce of the United States with the countries on this continent and adjacent islands for the year ended June 30, 1869.

[Compiled from the Annual Report on Commerce and Navigation.]

Countries.	Imports.	Exports.	Re-exports.	Total exports.	Total commerce.
Dominion of Canada	$30, 353, 010	$18, 188, 613	$2, 858, 782	$21, 047, 395	$51, 400, 405
All other British possessions in North America	1, 737, 304	2, 703, 173	446, 664	3, 149, 837	4, 887, 141
British West Indies	6, 682, 391	9 142, 344	101, 760	9, 244, 104	15, 926, 495
Total	38, 772, 705	30, 034, 130	3, 407, 206	33, 441, 336	72, 214, 041
Cuba	58, 201, 374	12, 643, 955	7, 064, 787	19, 708, 742	77, 910, 116
Porto Rico	7, 407, 900	2, 669, 964	114, 037	2, 784, 001	10, 191, 901
Total	65, 609, 274	15, 313, 919	7, 178, 824	22, 492, 743	88, 102, 017
French possessions in America	696, 952	1, 174, 056	45, 514	1, 219, 570	1, 916, 522
Danish West Indies	638, 550	1, 500, 000	39, 121	1, 539, 121	2, 177, 671
Dutch West Indies and Guiana	999, 099	926, 051	29, 595	955, 646	1, 954, 745
Hayti and San Domingo	729, 632	1, 349, 438	129, 462	1, 478, 900	2, 208, 532
Sandwich Islands	1 298, 065	700, 962	86, 665	787, 627	2, 085, 712
Total	4, 362, 318	5, 650, 507	330 357	5, 980, 864	10, 343, 182
Mexico	7, 232, 006	3, 836, 699	1, 047, 408	4, 884, 107	12, 116, 113
Central American States	733, 296	1, 324, 336	52, 146	1, 376, 482	2, 109, 778
Colombia	5, 291, 706	4, 900, 075	180, 267	5, 080, 342	10, 372, 048
Peru	1, 386, 310	1, 556, 434	116, 911	1, 673, 445	3, 059, 755
Chili	1, 186, 982	1, 969, 580	115, 905	2, 085, 485	3 272, 467
Argentine Republic	5, 162, 966	2, 235, 089	272, 425	2, 507, 514	7, 670, 480
Uruguay	1, 472, 608	835, 112	58, 270	894, 382	2, 366, 990
Brazil	24, 912, 450	5, 910, 565	158, 514	6, 069, 079	30, 981, 529
Venezuela	2, 431, 760	1, 191, 888	29, 176	1, 221, 064	3, 652, 824
Total	49, 810, 084	23, 760, 878	2, 031, 022	25, 791, 900	75, 601, 984
Grand total	158, 554, 381	74, 759, 434	12, 947, 409	87, 706, 843	246, 261, 224
Total commerce of United States	437, 314, 255	413, 954, 615	25, 173, 414	439, 128, 029	876, 442, 284

Imports and exports of Great Britain with Spanish America and some of the West India Islands for parts of the years 1868 *and* 1869.

	Year.	Imports.	Exports.
Cuba and Porto Rico	1869	£3, 228, 292	£1, 374, 242
French possessions in America	1868	4, 252	3, 002
Danish West Indies	1868	295, 102	9, 211
Dutch West Indies and Guiana	1868	148, 882	4, 444
Hayti and San Domingo	1868	220, 806	6, 043
Sandwich Islands	1868	33, 336	917
Mexico	1868	350, 664	92, 077
Central American states	1868	939, 827	173, 611
Colombia	1869	971, 396	2, 500, 039
Peru	1869	2, 734, 784	1, 180, 931
Chili	1869	3, 211, 174	1, 596, 905
Argentine Republic	1869	1, 034, 445	1, 841, 953
Uruguay	1869	535, 015	1, 009, 425
Brazil	1869	7, 754, 526	5, 477, 439
Venezuela	1868	69, 997	10, 452

www.ingramcontent.com/pod-product-compliance
Lightning Source LLC
LaVergne TN
LVHW020642110826
845149LV00004B/1318

* 9 7 8 1 4 1 8 1 9 0 7 6 7 *